P9-AGN-806

COLORFUL
LONDON

COLLINS

This edition published in Canada 1984 by Collins Publishers,
    100 Lesmill Road, Don Mills, Ontario.
© 1984 Illustrations and text: Colour Library Books Ltd.,
    Guildford, Surrey, England.
Display and text filmsetting by Acesetters Ltd.,
    Richmond, Surrey, England.
Printed and bound in Barcelona, Spain.
by JISA-RIEUSSET and EUROBINDER.
All rights reserved
ISBN 0-00-217232-1

"Earth has not anything to show more fair:
Dull would he be of soul who could pass by
A sight so touching in its majesty:
This City now doth like a garment wear

The beauty of the morning: silent, bare,
Ships, towers, domes, theatres, and temples lie
Open unto the fields, and to the sky,
All bright and glittering in the smokeless air."

Upon Westminster Bridge
(William Wordsworth)

Wordsworth's "mighty heart" of London is still there. Capital of Great Britain, it is a city which acts as the political, industrial and commercial centre of this majestic land, and was once the hub of the largest empire ever known. Its pre-eminence stems from its past: so many famous people have walked its streets; history weaves a rich tapestry through the ages and the story begins nearly two thousand years ago, back in Roman times...

Londinium was founded on the north side of the strategically important River Thames by the Roman invaders. However, they found that the fighting spirit of the native people was hard to crush: Boadicea, Queen of the Iceni – who occupied East Anglia – led an army which sacked the city. Eventually defeated in battle, she took her own life by poison in AD 62. Today, near the Houses of Parliament, a statue shows the warrior queen in her chariot with blades like scythes flashing from the wheel hubs. On the plinth beneath is enscribed the words, 'Regions Caesar never knew thy posterity shall sway'.

Take a walk nearer to the Palace of Westminster and there you will see the statue of a man who, throughout the darkest days of London, stood against the enemy's overwhelming forces; Sir Winston Churchill. Above him stands the clockface known as 'Big Ben', although it is really the 13½-ton bell within that was named after Sir Benjamin Hall and whose chimes are heard on BBC radio throughout the world. Nearby is Westminster Abbey, where the Kings and Queens of England have been crowned since William the Conqueror. It is also the burial place of the famous and includes Poet's Corner in the south transept, as well as the Tomb of the Unknown Soldier.

In Whitehall you come to the Cenotaph, memorial to the dead of both World Wars. Further on the left is Downing Street, the home of the Prime Minister, and you will see Horse Guards as well before you arrive at Trafalgar Square. This is dominated by Nelson's Column and Landseer's lions, and the National Gallery with its wide selection of the world's great masters: the vibrant sunflowers and corn fields of Van Gogh; the elaborate garden of Monet; the English countryside of Constable; the Venetian waterways of Canaletto; the coloured light of Turner and many other favourites.

Perhaps by now you will be feeling exhausted. But walk just a little way up Charing Cross Road and turn left into Soho. Here you can find a cosy wine bar or coffee shop in which to recuperate. Now the evening's entertainment may begin. The narrow, bustling streets throng with people and bright lights shine. Restaurants, theatres, night clubs and cinemas abound in this most cosmopolitan of areas. Tomorrow there will be time for more of London's attractions: St Paul's Cathedral designed by Sir Christopher Wren; Buckingham Palace, home of the Royal Family; shopping in Oxford Street or at Harrods; Speakers' Corner in Hyde Park where anyone can stand on a soapbox to speak their mind; a visit to the Tower of London, or perhaps to see one of the many museums.

This colourful book brings refreshing views of the capital city, with vivid photographs showing the vitality and variety of life in London. As Samuel Johnson wrote, "When a man is tired of London he is tired of life; for there is in London all that life can afford".

Previous page: the Albert Memorial, erected in 1876 in memory of the Prince Consort. This page: (above) Nelson's Column. (Top right) the Post Office Tower. (Right) County Hall on the South Bank. Opposite page: (top) Waterloo Bridge. (Bottom) the Houses of Parliament and the Clock Tower.

Opposite page: (top left) gazing resolutely across Parliament Square stands the statue of Sir Winston Churchill by Ivor Roberts-Jones. (Bottom left) Nelson's Column, Trafalgar Square. At the base of the column are four bronze reliefs, cast from captured French cannons, which show scenes from the naval battles which made Nelson a national hero: St Vincent, Copenhagen, The Nile and Trafalgar. (Right) Trafalgar Square and its spouting fountains. This page: (below) Landseer's lions, which surround the foot of the column, were cast from cannon recovered from the wreck of the *Royal George* which sank at Spithead in 1782. (Left) the Houses of Parliament and Westminster Bridge seen at night.

Opposite page: (top left) St Paul's Cathedral and *HMS Discovery*, taken to the Antarctic in 1900 by Captain Scott. (Top right) the White Tower of the Tower of London. (Centre left) Lambeth Bridge and the Houses of Parliament. (Centre right) Richmond Bridge. (Bottom left) Tower Bridge. (Bottom right) view from the National Westminster Tower. This page: (left and below) the Thames. (Bottom) St Katherine's Dock and Tower Hotel.

Opposite page: (top left) in Portsmouth Street is the 16th-century building made famous by Charles Dickens in his book *The Old Curiosity Shop*. (Top right) inside the department store of Selfridges. (Bottom) Oxford Street; prime shopping area for tourist and native Londoner alike. This page: (far left and left) there are many open-air markets in the city where all manner of bargains may be obtained. (Top) the scene around Petticoat Lane Market.

Opposite page: (top) the city skyline. (Bottom) the Houses of Parliament. This page: (Bottom left) Trafalgar Square. (Left) Dockland. (Bottom right) London bobby. (Below) the Clock Tower.

These pages: on special ceremonial occasions, such as Trooping the Colour, the regiments of Guards may be seen resplendent in their scarlet and black uniforms. The metal and leather accoutrements of the soldiers gleam as they march and ride in proud precision. They protect the London home of the Queen – Buckingham Palace (above) – where the ceremony of Changing the Guard may be seen daily. The knowledgeable can differentiate between Grenadier, Coldstream, Scots, Irish and Welsh Guards by the different spacing of their brass tunic buttons. Opposite page: (centre left) Queen Elizabeth II takes the salute of her soldiers.

Opposite page: the dome and cross of St Paul's Cathedral rise high above the gilded River Thames, dominating the buildings around. This page: (top left) Tower Bridge looms out of the grey mist. (Top right) the setting sun stains a golden path across the river as it wends its way through the heart of the city. (Above) illuminated Chelsea Bridge. Up river from London's centre, near Kew, is the hamlet of Strand-on-the-Green (far left). Richmond-upon-Thames (centre left and left) is the site of an old royal palace.

Opposite page: (top left) outside Buckingham Palace after the wedding of Prince Charles to Lady Diana. (Top right) Londoners pride themselves on setting the latest fashions. (Bottom) rain fails to deter shoppers in Oxford Street. This page: (top left) members of the Society of Toastmasters drink to Prince Charles and Diana. (Centre left and above) bobbies on the beat. (Left) pensioners of the Royal Hospital, Chelsea.

This page: (top) the White Tower is the oldest part of the Tower of London, dating from about 1078. (Right) wardens of the Tower of London. Opposite page: (top left) the Law Courts in the Strand. (Top right) known as The Monument, this pillar was built in 1672-1677 to commemorate the Great Fire of London of 1666, which devastated two-thirds of the capital in the course of five days. (Bottom left) part of the old Roman city wall, built at the end of the second century AD. (Bottom right) St Paul's Cathedral viewed from Cardinal Cap Alley, across the River Thames.

This page: (top left) Buckingham Palace. (Centre left) the Royal Festival Hall. (Top right) the Royal Albert Hall. (Above and right) Westminster Abbey. Opposite page: traffic in Whitehall. The light which burns in the Clock Tower shows that Parliament is sitting. By day, a Union Jack flying above the Victoria Tower of the Palace of Westminster – usually called the Houses of Parliament – demonstrates the same.

Opposite page: Piccadilly Circus. This page: (top left) Regent Street. (Top right) the statue of Eros, erected in 1893, actually represents the Angel of Christian Charity. (Centre right) Fleet Street. (Far left and left) the street markets of London, like Petticoat Lane and Portobello Road, bustle with life. (Above) Covent Garden provides fine shopping.

This page: (above) the Thames, coloured a delicate shade of mauve. (Top right) the Bank of England and Royal Exchange. (Centre right) each day, the population of London increases dramatically as commuters arrive for work by car, train and tube.

(Right) the National Westminster Tower is the tallest building in London and is 600 feet high with 52 floors. (Below) Fleet Street, famous as the 'Street of Ink'. Opposite page: Paddington Station, which provides train services to the west.

Opposite page: a member of the
Scots Guards. This page: (top
left) Welsh Guards. The regiment
suffered tragedy at Bluff Cove
in the Falkland Islands. Also
present during the campaign were
soldiers of the Blues and Royals
(above), who are distinguished
during ceremonial occasions by
their blue tunics and red
plumes. (Left) lunch-time music
from a military band in St
James's Park. (Below) mounted
policemen are a common sight.

Opposite page: the aerial photograph demonstrates that London contains many areas of restful parks and greens. St James's Park and Green Park can be seen set amid the grand buildings of Whitehall and The Mall, at the end of which is Buckingham Palace. Red buses scurry around Parliament Square and the panorama stretches out to the far horizon. This page: (top left) Regent's Park Canal. (Far left and left) riding or resting, Hyde Park is a lovely place to visit. (Above) within Kew Gardens, world famous for its collection of plants and trees, and its scientific research. (Top right) Old Deer Park, Richmond, scene of the last known duel in England.

This page: (above) barges being towed past Millbank Tower, towards Lambeth, Westminster, Hungerford and Waterloo Bridges. (Below) the lightship *Nore* in St Katherine's Dock. (Right) Richmond-upon-Thames. It was here that Queen Elizabeth I died in the royal palace. Her last words were, 'All my possessions for a moment of time'. Opposite page: the tide goes out, the sun goes down, and the Thames is bathed in golden light.

This page: some of the wonderful pubs of London. As Samuel Johnson said, 'There is nothing which has been contrived by man by which so much happiness is produced as by a good tavern or inn'. (Above) the Old Bull and Bush between Hampstead and Golders Green. (Right) outside Solange's wine bar after a wedding. (Bottom right) the Wheatsheaf. (Below) The Flask, in Highgate, was frquented long ago by Dick Turpin, the infamous highwayman, and later, by William Hogarth, the engraver and painter. Opposite page: Regent's Park Canal.

Opposite page: a London sunset seen in glorious shades of purple and blue. This page: (left) an official in the Palace of Westminster. (Bottom left) the Wellington Arch, Hyde Park Corner, is surmounted by a bronze chariot (far left) driven by a figure representing Peace. (Bottom right) the Post Office Tower. (Below) Trafalgar Square.

Opposite page: (top) the White Tower. (Bottom left) cycling in the rain. (Bottom right) the Cenotaph war memorial in Whitehall. This page: (top left) the Yeomen of the Guard, a body formed by Henry VII in 1485. (Above) British bobbies; famed throughout the world. (Left) a vendor of London's evening newspaper, *The Standard*. (Below) Westminster Abbey.

This page: (top left) the neon lights of Piccadilly Circus. (Centre left) Lambeth Bridge and the Houses of Parliament (top right). (Above) the Post Office Tower. (Right) the Royal Festival Hall. Opposite page: (top) Hampton Court Palace, built by Cardinal Wolsey in 1515. (Bottom) the riverside on the South Bank.

This page: examples of the many scenes that London conjures to the mind. (Above) the 'clippie' on the bus. (Right) cricket on the green. (Below) open-air fruit market. (Centre right) bewigged barristers. (Bottom right) a Yeoman Warder.

This page: (left) a military band plays at the bandstand in Hyde Park. (Bottom left) mews cottages in Hampstead. (Below) the statue of Peter Pan – the boy who never grew up – in Kensington Gardens. (Bottom right) the intricate design on the Albert Memorial.

Previous pages: the pomp and precision of the Guards regiments. This page: (top left and centre right) the cool verdancy of London's parks and gardens. (Top right) St James's Park. (Above) Windsor Castle was originally built by William the Conqueror to protect the western approaches to London and is, today, a residence of the Queen. (Right) the ornamental gates which lead into Queen Mary's Garden, Regent's Park. Opposite page: Hampton Court Palace was given to Henry VIII in 1526 and remained a royal residence until the time of George III.

These pages: in the light of dawn or dusk, reflected from the waters of the Thames or seen through the enveloping mists of morning, London is a city of grandeur, its very stones echoing the remorseless passage of time. Opposite page: (top left) a silhouetted bronze griffin marks Temple Bar and the City boundary. It replaced a gate upon which, until 1745, the heads of executed villains were set as an example to any who might have cared to follow the path of the criminal.

This page: (top) the turrets and towers of the Palace of Westminster etched against the sky at dusk. (Above) Oxford Street. (Right and opposite page: left) the Clock Tower. (Centre right) Lambeth Bridge. (Top right and bottom right) a misty reminder of the days of 'peasouper' fogs.

This page: (right) Tower Bridge. (Above, below and opposite page: top) St Paul's Cathedral. (Bottom left) the statue of Boadicea near the Clock Tower. (Centre left) 'Justice' above the Old Bailey. (Centre right) choristers in the Tower of London. (Bottom right) Trafalgar Square's Christmas tree is presented each year by Norway.

These pages: the National Gallery, its neo-Palladian facade overlooking the north side of Trafalgar Square. Its collection of paintings comprehensively covers the major periods in the history of art. This page: (right) detail from *Madonna and Child with St John the Baptist and St Jerome* by Parmigianino (Girolamo Francesco Maria Mazzola)(1503-1540). He was one of the most sensitive painters among the early Mannerists. (Far right) *St Catherine of Alexandria* by Raphael (Raffaello Santi)(1483-1520). Opposite page: (top left) *Flower-piece*, by Paul Gauguin (1848-1903), was painted in Tahiti during 1896. (Top right) *The Morning Walk* by Thomas Gainsborough (1727-1788). (Bottom left) *Susanna Lunden, 'Le Chapeau de Paille'* by Peeter Pauwel Rubens (1577-1640). (Bottom right) *The Fighting Téméraire* by Joseph Mallord William Turner (1775-1851). He was a Londoner, born in Maiden Lane, Covent Garden.

These pages: one of the attractions of an evening in London is a visit to the theatre or ballet. The city has, of course, been famous for its production of plays for centuries and, encouraged under the patronage of Elizabeth I, 'The Theatre' was built in Shoreditch in 1576 by John Burbage. 'The Globe' in Southwark was opened in 1598 by Richard Burbage and became famous for the literary genius who walked its boards; William Shakespeare. Ballet brings together the separate and distinct art forms of dancing, drama, music and painting. Although its origins lie in Classical Greece, the form as we know it today developed in the Court of King Louis XIV.

Opposite page: (top) the Queen's House, Greenwich – in the centre of the picture – was built for Anne of Denmark and, upon her death, for the wife of Charles I; Henrietta Maria. The colonnades link it to the National Maritime Museum. (Bottom) Buckingham Palace and St James's Park, through which Charles I walked, from St James's Palace to Horse Guards, on his way to the block. This page: (far left) the Pagoda in Kew Gardens. (Left) Richmond-upon-Thames. (Below) schoolgirls near Sloane Street. (Bottom) Kenwood House, Hampstead.

This page: (below and right) the
Bank of England, on the left,
and the beautiful facade of the
Royal Exchange. (Bottom) the
crypt chapel of St Stephen's in
the Palace of Westminster.
Opposite page: (top left) the
clipper *Cutty Sark* in dry dock
at Greenwich. (Remaining
pictures) St Paul's Cathedral.

This page: (right) a Guard stands lonely vigil. (Bottom and far right) the Houses of Parliament and the Clock Tower. The statue is of Jan Christiaan Smuts. Opposite page: (top) the Queen Victoria Memorial, outside Buckingham Palace, with The Mall leading away to Admiralty Arch. (Top right) Horse Guards in Whitehall. (Bottom left) the Royal Staircase in the Houses of Parliament and (bottom right) the Robing Room. The painting shows Christ and Sir Galahad, the knight who could sit in the Siege Perilous of King Arthur's Round Table without risk of his life and who succeeded in the quest of the Holy Grail.

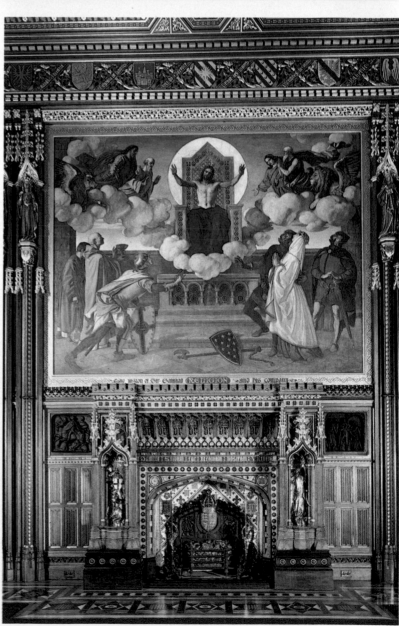

This page: (above and top left) Sotheby's, the auctioneers, were established in 1744. (Top right) Egyptian Hall, Mansion House. (Right) the Whale Hall in the Natural History Museum. Opposite page: Apsley House, once the home of the Duke of Wellington. Overleaf: a flower seller.